The Toy Box

The Toy Box

Mike Johnson

99% Press,
an imprint of Lasavia Publishing Ltd.
Auckland, New Zealand

www.lasaviapublishing.com

Copyright © Mike Johnson, 2020

This book is copyright. Apart from any fair dealing for the purpose of private study, research, criticism or reviews, as permitted under the Copyright Act, no part may be reproduced by any process without the permission of the publishers.

Much thanks to Leila Lees for cover artwork, Jennifer Rackham for cover design, Neil Sonnekus for proof-reading and Daniela Gast for layout and overall book design,

ISBN: 978-0-9951282-0-0

The Soul

In Queen Street
on Friday night
– lights blooming but
already pomegranate-heavy
with Adult Entertainment –
a yellow balloon
was hopping around
among herds of cars,
holding its helium soul together,
two lives left,
to the music of singing ironclads,
hopping, filled with its yellow
balloon-fright
before wheels
and behind wheels
incapable of salvation
incapable of destruction,
one life left,
half a life left,
with a molecular trace of helium,

using its last resources
its string searching
for some child's hands
Sunday morning

Miroslav Holub

Translated by Dana Hábová
And David Young

Part One

into the toy box

the first page

the first page opens
                a staircase
                            into the
turning world
      of the toy box
with all its bits and bobs
and happenstance

toys that sit
toys that don't
pieces that fit
pieces that won't
and pieces that belong
to quite another puzzle

there goes Jack Horner and Little Boy Blue
across the gutter and
around the corner of the illustration
into the everyday street
where everyone walks
spits their hopes and fears
and buys toys for the kids
at that time of the year

they look the same
as everybody else with somewhere to go
even if it's let's-pretend
and there's lots of let's-pretend
to go around

walk for long enough and you will find Margery Door
still on her see-saw, Mother Goose amid
gigabytes of mountains and imaginations
and you might like to grab
a quick snack with the Muffin Man
down in Drury Lane

a nice way to finish the day
in toy land

you can see all this stuff as the morning grows
easy as turning a new leaf
opening a vein
or wandering in the forever afternoon, climbing the
Faraway Tree, trying not to wonder why
as the shadows climb up after you
anyone would want to bake
four-and-twenty blackbirds in their feathers
still dreaming of flightless skies

a house with no windows

they made a house out of bricks and sand
and sticky stuff
but forgot to put in the windows

the man in the moon was sad
because he had no nice glass to shine through

so he went to ask the jade rabbit
who'd been digging holes in the moon
for all eternity (it's easy to see them!)
to ask for advice

you can't ask me, the rabbit said, because
I dig burrows and burrows don't have
windows, silly – deep underground there is a burrow heaven
and it has no windows

so the man in the moon visited the woodcutter
who worked alone in the dark, cutting down
an acacia tree, which healed itself
after every blow of his silver axe

you can't ask me, the woodcutter said
I have no time, I'm too busy to look around
and can only see your light
in the blade of my axe

so the man in the moon went to the goddess who lives
in the mountains of the moon
in a splendid palace of ice

you can't ask me, she said, I've been
banished from the earth forever
because I stole my king's elixir
and so a house without windows
is just like my heart, all closed off
and shut away

this made the man in the moon even sadder:
        he couldn't shine in the rabbit's burrow
        he could only shine on the woodcutter's blade
        he couldn't shine in the goddess's heart
        he couldn't even shine on the foolish toys
who forgot to put windows in their houses
of bricks and sand and sticky stuff

but there was love in his heart, even for the poor
chipped and broken toys with their eyes rubbed out
and their houses with no windows, no doors even,
so he turned his sad face away, to the other side, the dark side
where the stars alone could see his tears
and his bright and happy face might always
be looking our way

the story bag

it's a cloth bag
drawn tight with a blue drawstring
heavy with stories
all in different shapes
weights and colours

the word made flesh
the flesh made word
the word made king
the king made queen
and everything between

stories for all ages and rages
from pins to pumpkins
from cats to cages
snake and fox

stories of loss and of gain
whole or in part
old or fresh

here's a piece of jade
that fell from the moon
still glowing
and turned the sea green

here's pearl of ancient rain
locked in swamp gum

this one is a starfish
a long way from memories of the sea
and the circular swing of the galaxy

this one a ceramic blowfish
that doubles as a whistle
(you blow through the tail)

and here's a piece of plaid
paper thin, with a yellowy look
your grandmother must have added
as a little domestic touch

plus one bird's nest
in a green flame

and here's a seed
from deep space, reddy-brown
shaped like a heart

some are warm to the touch
some have faces
some are lost in time
some spurn love, some seek fame

some hide away in shame
and some build houses
and some tear them down

some are, probably,
most decidedly, not true
while others make their own
arrangements with verisimilitude

it's a lot for a little cloth bag
drawn tight with a blue drawstring
a lot of whispering
in even the darkest of places

stories spilling out
into the toy box

the truth about the rescue of the story bag

Anansi
the floppy spider with green eyes,
spun a thread to heaven
to rescue the story bag
from the fearsome sky god
Nyame
who had taken all the stories of the world
for himself
to have and to hoard
forever and a day

humanity had grown sad
without its stories; children
couldn't sleep at night, the stars
forgot to shine
and even dogs lost
their bone-hill dreams

nobody knew where to go
or what to do
or even why they should
get up the morning
or go to bed at night

it was as if all the stories of the world
had died
and left no marker of their passing

Nyame set Anansi three impossible tasks
but spidy would have none of that

he'd heard of those kinds of deals before
the story bag was full of them
dangerous situations
heroics required in every case
along with wit, wisdom
and dedication

where truth lies
stories too are spun like silken threads
from the inflated fantasies
of clever, tricker gods

but the truthful truth is that Anansi
got Nyame drunk with a special potion
containing spider venom
which caused his majesty to fall in love
with his second cousin
and in the confusion Anansi stole
the story bag and spiralled back to earth
with all the stories of the world

safe and sound

even this one

for the special enjoyment of our ears

our ears, our ears

Scheherazade: a still life

the picture shows
a young woman on an embroidered cushion
sitting in front of her king

she looks very composed

the king lounges back, one knee up
an arm resting loosely upon it
the other hand holding a hookah
from which there arises spirals and
curlicues and fairy rings

in the background attendants hover

by his side a scimitar
with a curved moon blade
and an ornate guard
lies negligently
on the folds of his royal gown

the king looks very composed
the hookah looks very dignified
the spirals and curlicues and fairy rings
are fantastical

the attendants are suitably awed

and the scimitar looks as if it were dreaming
perhaps of a red satin cushion
in a palace of peace
with the burbling call of doves
and the quiver of water in cool stone pools
where rainbow coloured fish flick
from instant to instant

she is leaning forwards, one hand raised flat
palm up
as if she were offering him a delicacy
on a plate, her head tilted up a little
her mouth open

words! I know she needs words
I would love to help her with some
words love to be needed
or they go brown and die like fallen leaves

but it's more than words she needs
it's a special magic, a story magic
as each word awaits the next
most breathlessly
and events can hardly keep pace
with themselves

meanwhile, the king keeps smoking his hookah
with spirals and curlicues and fairy rings

the attendants hover expectantly

and the scimitar keeps dreaming
of vanquished foes,
of an exalted future in the Hand of God
as the greatest sword of all time
with the sharpest blade of all time
the sword of swords

a proud blade that would never
stoop to beheading a girl like this
this particular girl, in fact
who speaks so sweetly, whose only crime
is innocence
and to have to feel once more
sticky human blood along the blade

the picture shows
a scene of opulent tranquility
but everybody knows
even the gloating attendants

where the story must end

the pop-up ballerina

the music box hasn't been opened
for a very long time
its hinges are stiff

the pop-up ballerina
has had no chance to pop up
and whirl around
to a tinkle-dinkle version
of twinkle-twinkle little star
or Fűr Elise
or Chopin's Nocturne

no chance to captivate
even for a moment
with visions of impossible purity
and rinky-dink sweetness
the sunlit nursery
the moonlit nursery
the moment of magic in the toy box
the suspension of disbelief
when imaginings become plangent
the pace brisk
before the slow winding down
plink by
plonk

the long wait for the next note
the final moment of incredulity
when everything stops

the music box hasn't been opened
since the last nostalgic moment
and nobody knows if the music still plays
or if the ballerina will appear
and make a comeback
but everyone is keeping fingers crossed
for in that moment, that silly pink
and twirly moment
we might be ourselves, as at the very first
when the spring is wound up
tight
the tune fresh
and the ballerina takes the stage

narratives on the run

1
one fine day
(in the middle of the night)
they loosened the drawstring and
out of the story bag they came
all in a rush
narratives on the loose
impatient
bursting with words
leaping into what they hoped
was the bright light
or any kind of light
leaving the old and the tired dark
behind

there isn't a narrative that doesn't dream
of freedom
in its heart of hearts

but it was kind of crowded and dim
in the toy box
with so many soft-machine dreams
jostling around
that the stories had nowhere much to go
no secure place

no cyber-protected soapbox
no home in the eye of a friendly reader
and nobody much to admire them

so they took to the four directions
heedless
and in search of true gods
and divine fonts

2
it wasn't long before Anansi gave the alarm
and the hunt was on
hither and yon, high and low
here and beyond the lexicon and the
phonemes of desire

even the humans joined in
the little girl in red gumboots
with some of the bolder toys
Big Ted and Little Ed
Noddy, and the girls from the cowboy band
searched together all around
here and there, under the sofa
behind the fridge
on top of old smoky
beside running waters
and the inside of buckets with crenellations
for making sand castles

you never know where a story might hide
or syllables stashed

the stories were not to be found
neither within nor without
above or below
and a great wordless wailing shook the world

perhaps the skygod has come down
from his lofty heights
and stolen the stories from
under our tongues again
people said

they searched under their tongues
interrogated their voice boxes
squeezed their lungs
and made a great fuss before heaven

turned the toy box upside down
and shook the world from side to side
before everyone got seasick

3
from the stories' point of view
being out of the bag was not all
it was cracked up to be
there were no cheering crowds

no laurels to wear or sit on
no handsome volumes seeking them out
no handmade paper, with marbled end-pages
and crafted leather spines
awaited their pleasure

it was dusty under the sofa
it was cramped behind the fridge
and all the other places had problems
problems! problems!
it was no better in the kitchen
behind the pots and pans
or in the great metaphysical beyond
where abstractions ruled
and narratives pined away

some became so depressed
they lost their cutting edge
or devised gloomy endings
no reader would care to stomach

others had grimmer fates

still others dreamed of dissolving
back into the Great Dictionary
in the hope of being reborn again
sometime

eventually peace was declared, since stories
are made for ears, big and little
flesh and fabric, plain or plastic
there is no better place
to rehearse their lines
than the nice, snug, welcoming
story bag

Noddy – a short story

not fair to say that Noddy is the dumbarse of Toy Town
although his bell does a fair amount of jingling
on top of his spring-loaded head
to little effect

and he is a tad too easily frightened

Big Ears too has come under a lot of flack
for being a hearty know-nothing
with an overfondness for platitudes
and a suspicious attachment
to the little wooden toy with the dunce's hat
the painted smile
and the helpless noddy-nod-nod of his little head

those toy-town gossips will never understand
the true nature of bromance

in fact, everybody takes care of the little
nodding man – he never comes to any harm –
and Mr Plod, a cop of immeasurable slowness
of speech, always remembers what Noddy's house
looks like even when Noddy himself
has forgotten

once he went to Big Ears' house thinking
that he was Big Ears
they had a lot of muddily sorting out to do
after which they sat down for a nice cup of tea

not the squarest block in the box, but getting there
and look, he has his own little yellow car with the
blue fenders, he's coming along just fine
is Noddy
thank you very much
and never forget that, like you and me
and everybody else in the box,
he too was made by Old Man Carver

the tale of Wee Ted and the pumpkin seeds

it was all the doing of the littlest toy
in the box – Wee Ted
(with the smallest bed)
who set out
searching for the beans
that might float him all the way up
to the land of the big people
where Old Man Carver lives
and as every toy knows, Old Man Carver
is the author of many a rocking horse
and every little wooden toy from here
to kingdom come

now Wee Ted was none too smart
his head was made of soft stuff
his limbs were even softer
while his eyes were crosses of black thread
frayed

he wasn't much good outside the toy box
thinking the floor was the ceiling
the ceiling was the walls
and walls were some impossible

horizon line

that windows were square moons
and that Old Man Carver might live on top
of the kitchen table or in the linen cupboard

and nothing had prepared him for real mice

he found his magic beans which of course
were not beans but who's to say - if Wee Ted
thinks they're beans then they have
a fair chance of being beans
despite their determined pumpkinness
their shape and smell

beaniness is in the eye of the beholder
in this case a button eye

they may not put down roots into the dust
at the bottom of the toy box
or scale the heights of air to the land
of the big people
but they are just great at playing let's pretend
with the littlest toy in the box
and even a pumpkin might one day
turn into a magic bean
and grow and grow
and grow

the colouring book

the colouring-in book remains
mostly uncoloured
with a few zig-zag crayon marks
at random
and occasionally
a green or yellow head
or lavender shoes
or a dog with a blue tongue
or dirty marks where little fingers tried
to claw out the sun

there's a pig with spectacles
reading *The Times*
with red blobs for hands
Sunday blue for eyes not quite fixed
in their frame
and a golden arrow
where his heart should be

there's Mary Mouse with her broom
tackling armies of dust, the broom
having got ahead of itself, its own
purple patch yet to be swept
has been cancelled by some black crosses
running from gutter to corner
never intended to colour anything

she's an extreme case

Mr Plod blowing his whistle
under a crayon-bruised sky
has a touch of orange on each knee
and his face has been reshaped
to look like a pumpkin
with mauve dots
and an amber antenna
a Plod from outer space

some serious intent here

and so it goes for every page
you'll have to look for yourself
if you want more of the same
page after page
hectically turned with a few
rubs and slashes and furry balls
looks like it was all used up
in a single day
a single hour

its cover now torn
pages stuck together
by lumps of coloured grease
not quite ready for the scrap heap

not quite used up, it remains
misused

a wasted world of black lines
some capricious god
could never bring into being
or quite believe in
but could happily scribble over

the fork and spoon tango

when the fork ran away with the spoon
there was a great ta-doo in the toy box

you can read all about in the *Fairy Tale Times*

the truth is that nobody sang
hey diddle diddle (as if they would!)
the little dog did not laugh
to see such craft, the notion of a cow
jumping over the moon
was patently ridiculous
and the cat and the fiddle
would have nothing to do with it
full stop

shame on the FTT for spreading
false news stories, and hyping
what was a most personal
and painful matter, an unlikely love affair
of the most haunting kind

the disappearance of the fork and the spoon
is that much more mysterious
given their mutual embarrassment
on discovering

that they were in love
and no amount of rattling of the cutlery drawer
would change that

in the normal world forks want to fork
and spoons want to spoon
and in this way the natural order is maintained
but when the world gets turned over
and inside out
by love
a fork may want to spoon
and a spoon may want to fork
without rhyme or reason
so who are we to mock
or question
the great spoonfork
of the universe
which may burst in upon us
in our forkedness and spoonness
and send us
scratching against the walls of the toy box

the FTT's fanciful little tale
might be fine for children to sing
and perhaps no one has to know
the tragedy lurking in the ditty
the humiliation of the hey diddle diddle
or has to wonder

what became of them

if they are clinking together

somewhere

or are far far far

far apart

a good old sing-song

once a month or so
everybody stands around the piano
and has a good old sing-song
just like the old days

dressed in their Sunday best
the toys come
and if they don't remember all the words
it doesn't matter
because someone else does
and as long as they all sway
back and forward in the same direction
everything goes pretty well

their voices will never soar to heaven
on the back of a descant
nor set the body quivering
with a touch of fire – Big Ted
looks as if he might be courting a stroke
with his mouth open and his face purple
but he's not one to shun the high notes
and Wee Ted will roll over backwards
to hit the bass

it's a bit like being in church except
you're allowed to laugh
when a note comes out wrong
or a word is forgotten
or a phrase misplaced
because of a lifetime spent not singing

the piano has seen better days
but so has everybody
so nobody cares too much
it doesn't so much play the notes
(which don't sound quite right)
as remember them from the honky-tonk
barroom years when the keys were called
ivories and the sounds held true
right to the dying fall
of sackcloth and sad songs
wars and reunions
loves and lost loves and loves
that never were

a lot of loves went marching off in a major key
while the minor keys stayed at home weeping
but the toys knew none of this
even those who sang the loudest
or with the most feeling

and the words… the words…
well the words are just something to sing
around the piano
after all

the little tractor

the little tractor has something wrong
with its wind-up heart

it went into stop-go mode
then stopped altogether

once it had some pretty fine action
whirring over a ploughed carpet
or chugging up the armrest of a settee
all by itself

a certain integrity of intention
you might say, a bit of the toughness
you might expect
from a little motor made to be tough
just like the big ones

some say its cogs got all graunched
so it couldn't be wound up
while others say that someone
lost the key
that's all
while still others maintain
it hit the wall

and its wheels kept grinding away
until it gave up hope

and now its wheels won't even turn

one day a child, a notional child,
will pick it up and skim it or grind it
over the carpet
but it won't be the same
only any good in fantasy land
where the child has to make
the *grum-grum* sound
any proud motor would make
given half a chance

the little tractor has something wrong
with its wind-up heart
and already it can feel the rust
corroding
its once mighty spring

visit the gift horse

don't pause to count the teeth
in the mouth of a gift horse
they say
among other things they say

there's a gift horse in the toy box
that will make your every wish come true
if you wish for it hard enough
they say

a sort of resident genie
in disguise
an ordinary enough looking gift horse
made of soft green stuff with a nice red coat
and proper ears sewn on
and a red mouth to match the coat
probably not many teeth
one doesn't like to ask
or look too hard

but this ordinary looking toy
has extraordinary gifts, beyond counting
beyond your wildest dreams
beyond all there is and will be
the gifts that go on giving
unheralded and unsung

if
you would you like to see a place
where the rich are made poor
and the poor can eat
and a mountain can float free
of the encumbrance of the earth
and all that is sick is made well
and all that is well is made divine
heart, blood and blood cell
and you don't have to worry
about what might happen if you get your wish
then
visit the gift horse
bearing your life in your hands like a beach ball
you can drop
and make your wish right there

and this little gift horse will get
right to work, changing the universe around
to suit your wishes, upending old regimes
and bringing in the wind
sorting out time and sequence
to make sense to the eye
and bringing some brave love
in from the cold

don't look a gift horse in the mouth
teeth or no teeth
they say
among other things they say

and there is wisdom in that
for the gift horse only comes around
once in a blue moon
with his fine red coat
and his sewn-on ears
and the power to move worlds

a place in the scheme of things

the Jack of Spades endures
its separation from the pack
with a stoical mien

desertion, abandonment, loss
absence from the hierarchy of meanings
or the order of angels
it regards with aplomb

loss of family and friends, rivals
and lovers
is harder to take
but who's counting?

fondly it remembers life on the shuffle
with all its cuzzie bros and colleagues
teasers and leavers
its place in the scheme of things
its skin in the game

it would no more
defy the ace than despise the ten
for it has no need
to reassure itself that the
mighty Jack of Spades

is just the card to be
when the chips are down

for in the fall of the cards it might find
the power of the bower
outrank even the cunning ace
turn a losing hand into a winning one
or complete a straight or flush

the One Eyed Jack, they call it
because the other eye is looking out into
another universe
no gambler can see
and dreams of plays no earthly player
can execute

we have to ask what it's doing
on the bottom of the toy box
face down
alone
nothing but the other eye
to see with

maybe the whole pack is scattered
to the four winds
the Jack the last left standing
against all odds

waiting for the game to resume
to be picked
and carefully positioned
to be loved again
to feel the weight of a greater fate

in some new game of chance

no stay of execution for the ditherers

in Toy Town
the jug is always full
but the bench is mostly empty
and everybody has either gone home
or yet to arrive

there's little room
for half-measures
or fuzzy in-betweens
false reassurances
or delayed effects

the jug is always empty
but the bench is mostly full
everybody has already arrived
or gone shopping

the jug sits upside down
on the table – nobody gets wet
nobody says anything that shouldn't be said
nothing has to be taken back
brought forward
or tabled for a vote

jug and bench make a perfect pair
one full, the other empty, one empty
the other full
they swap yarns on a Saturday night
and remember what the other forgets
which is a great way to do it
no questions asked
and nobody has to tell any lies

it's like that everywhere, the same jug
the same bench
the same eternal arrangement
people coming and going
threading
present and past
idea and form
time and circumstance

when all ambiguity is banished
the 'neither here nor there' crowd
get a short shrift

no stay of execution
for the ditherers
the fence sitters
the dollar-each-way crowd

jug and bench are empty and full
the people are alive or dead
god doesn't hesitate
Toy Town always gets its just deserts
one way or the other

the great leveler

it was a set-up from the start
the dolls were all lined up
their dresses crisp
their smiles identical
their deception immaculate
their price tags carefully hidden
unless on special

freshly unwrapped, cleared
of its cellophane cowl
the doll steps forward in all its glory
plastic hair gleaming
not a mark or scratch
the delicious smell of plastic
fresh off the assembly line

the clothes too, suitable
as evening wear, a cocktail party
or a restaurant where the waiters
wear bow ties
modest but classy
without a smudge or crinkle
there is nothing like
that first pristine moment
before anything happens

and destiny and fate and all
the other pretenders
throw their hats into the ring

of course you and I know that
without fail
the joy will wear off
the sequins will lose their glitter
and no matter how glad the rags
how grandiose the visions
or impeccable the pedigree
it's all pretty much the same
after a while

in the toy box

Goldilocks the refugee

she was little and sad and lost
had no home under the sun
and she'd come a long way
over some hard roads

perhaps she'd been cursed by a wicked fairy
or born to war and strife
in some place where it got too hot
and the rivers ran dry

there was dust on her dress,
her ankles were sore
and when a door opened up in a world
with the light too bright
she had no choice but to step through
into the cool interior
the shady spaces
of somebody else's home

the interloper

knowing
if she kept trying, there was a place
just for her, a world that fitted her
a place to eat and sleep

and dream, not of dog-faced soldiers
or burnt meadows
but a little house, in a wood
near a green, by rushing water
with a kindly teddy bear
watching over her sleep

that useless plastic tree

we'd agree
that a tiny plastic tree
like this one
is not much use to anybody
but for the most fleeting of attention
from some toddler
who's not fooled anyway
and is fast learning the difference
between things you can eat
and things you might choke on

yet there it is at the bottom of the toy box
more plastic than tree, so carelessly shaped
no particular tree springs to mind
just the most basic generic form
no attempt at branches, and
with little flaps of plastic left over
from the pressing

if you broke it in half
it wouldn't bleed

its base is so malformed
it will barely stand
but once it was placed somewhere

to lord it over an imaginary forest
full of lyrical, magical things
or mark a fancy boulevard
fit for kings or queens
in the tinpot dreams of Toy Town

now it's gathering dust
a useless hunk of junk
destined for some landfill
or some ocean – did it give
a moment's pleasure, could it ever
forget its rigid plasticness
its lumpish tragedy

its worse-than-uselessness?

they dance before the faithless

these little red shoes took her feet
on a merry dance
until her feet were gone
and even that couldn't stop them

feet or no feet
the dance goes on

laughter in the ballroom
songs in the meadows
weeping in the forest

the executioner lined up her legs
decided to chop her off at the knees
to make her more acceptable

for his sword he chose
the edge of the gibbous moon
a slice of darkness

she said her farewells
and bled into the stars

the little red shoes
still haunt the church
and dance before the faithless
most prettily

feet or no feet
girl or no girl
the dance goes on

prayers in the vestry
dirges in the meadows
arias on the bridges

you can hear the tap-tap-tapping
of the obscene rhymes, and the cries
of the orphans and their children
as counterpoint, contrapuntal

none have penetrated
to the secret heart of the girl
who couldn't stop dancing

the big bad wind blew into town

Toy Town clock tower
got knocked over by a big bad wind
nobody knew whether to laugh or cry
or just fall down

now time has lost its way
in the dark-dark woods
with no crumbs or white stones
to follow

the clock tower was never
much to write home about
it never aspired to touch
the hem of heaven
or become a beacon of hope
was never much use for anything
but for climbing up and down
the way the ants did
and it didn't offer much of a view
beyond the rim of the toy box

it would never have won
an architectural award
not even in the land of toys
where tottering towers teetered

on a regular basis
and the impermanence of all things
ruled

the big bad wind – that was something else
it didn't belong in the land of toys
it had no place in the story bag
it was never sewn into flags
or left behind in the dreamcatcher

it blew in from some other place

yet it woke the child
with the fall of a lonesome train whistle
disturbed the dreams of the dreamers
with the sound of giant footfalls
and a dire song
about the end of time

some saw it as a portent
some as an act of dog
some as a game of numbers
some as a joke
and some saw it
as way beyond the joke

but whatever it was or did or meant
it knocked down that little clock
tower
that had never done any harm

now time lies on its side
general confusion reigns
as everybody forgets what time it is
what day it is
and when they might die

and then the wicked fairy came

someone has cast a spell on the toy box
things ain't what they used to be

once there was lots of hurrying and scurrying
to-ing and fro-ing, and everybody was busy
keeping busy with something
important

if it weren't for all this keeping busy
there'd be nothing to do

Mrs Broom swept clean
Mr Brush swept dirty
in the children's room, the dance
of the feather duster and the fly swat
kept things lively
kept the dust on the move
and the smile on the face
of the smiley face

while the little electric engine that could
went around and around and aroundabout
and lost the four directions as east went west
and north went south
but nobody cared too much, hell,

it was party time even in the dark-dark woods
where the goblins live

then the wicked fairy came
if that's what it was
like a thief in the night
and touched the sky
and even the earth, and shook
all the creatures that live on the earth
even all the creepy-crawlies

and all those that were touched
lost themselves
and no longer knew the toy box
for what it was

now they look like they're moving
but they're only playing let's pretend
the hare and the bear sit down for tea
with buttons for scones
(one for you and two for me)
and laces for graces
but they're only playing let's pretend

Noddy and Big Ears go for a walk
have a little talk but nothing gets said
no words are spoken
because they're only playing let's pretend

things have never been the same
since the wicked fairy came
and cast its horrid spell

I wish I wish I wish
I could tell them
no spell lasts forever, friends
comrades of the toy box!
we have magicians working overtime
on the problem
and Mighty Mouse in the wings
always ready… steady
here I come to save the day!

where it goes, nobody knows

time's not the same in the toy box
it's more like playdough
or that gooey stuff you throw at walls
and it sticks… for a while

it can get a bit spooky
at night in the toy box
with nothing to comfort you
but the muddledy dreams of Raggedy Ann
in which time does a loop-de-loop
and comes back as the enemy
the steady march of the clock-tick

meanwhile some of the smarter toys
like Jiminy Cricket
have begun to suspect
that they are losing pieces of time
as surely as they are losing their stuffing
or the colour
off their once shiny paint jobs

but where time flows, nobody knows
and nobody knows how far it goes
or where it stops

time flakes off, the cricket said
and Pooh Bear agrees – he's seen
some pretty flaky time in his time
'not every pot of honey is equal in weight'
he says
which is really wise
for a bear of very little brain

Bob the Builder and the Bobsy Twins
wake up in a place where no time passes
everything hangs suspended
the clock stops, never to go again

the arrow at the bottom of the box
is frozen in mid-air, no nearer, no further away
from the target
which is nothing more than a face
in the hallows of memory

it's true, time is not the same in the toy box
it's gone all corkscrew
and put the toys into a coma

you'll know what's happened if you stare hard enough
into their blank faces
and listen for their absent whispers
in their world of lost words

no place for realism

in the toy box there is no birth
or death
although things do fall apart
and new things might arrive
fully made
at my given moment
out of nowhere

nobody has any babies
but there's lots of pretending
like Mrs Weathervane and her pram
or Peta Peatwater with her plastic womb
but smooth between the legs

the toy box is no place for realism
some details are best skipped over
imagination is required to turn
plastic into flesh and a hollow place
or stuffed space
into blood and bone

there may be a train station
or a police box, or a house
made out of blocks
but you won't see a funeral parlour

or a cemetery
because the area is strictly patrolled
by lead soldiers with muskets
brightly painted
whose job it is
to keep the outside separated from
the inside, and the above separated
from the below
so everybody can sleep happily at night
without having to worry

besides, friends, it's amazing what you
can patch up and cobble together
with a little needle and thread
not quite as grandiose as birth and death
perhaps
but it does the job
and gives some old comrades
a new lease of life

now you see me

the dreams of the toy box
are all of other places
far away from the paint-scratched
mishmash
of some very untidy toys

there are lots of clean white lines
and children-free spaces
lovely zen silences
and a somewhere over the rainbow

as well as beaches and beach balls
and cheeks as rosy as
and sunlit spaces
and plenty of places to play
now-you-see-me-now-you-don't
or
catch-me-if-you-can

there're hills too, real ones
with yellow tussock that holds fast
to the rocky ground
and mountains that creak and tremble
when the sky comes too close to dreams
and trucks that ruck and rumble
all the way into playtime

there are lots of big wide wonderful
open landscapes to run around in
and trees to climb with real branches
that break if you go too high
and real streams for pretend boats
and real birds to peck out your eyes
and a real meal on the table

the dreams of the toy box are not
of the toy box but very far away
as far as myth and makeshift will go
as far as memory and imagination
even to the edge of the great ocean
so great it has no horizon
and I would beware, if I were you
of loose talk about kapok dreams
or plastic dreams
or wooden dreams
or feather dreams
or the metal dreams
of tin soldiers

bashed, dented, kicked, chewed
and regularly upended
the pristine dreams of the toy box
become all we remember
and are

a troubling poignancy

toys will dream
that one day they will lose
their toyness
and turn into real little children
with inaugurations all their own

it is a desire filled with a troubling
poignancy
a disturbing sense of not belonging
of not being as real as everything else
of rejection and abandonment

of course toys don't think
about such things
overtly
or even feel such things
covertly
but
being made of wood and plastic and fluff
doesn't mean a toy can't
wake up with a peculiar pain
in the heart
or a memory that can be traced back
to before the invention of stars
or the writing of texts

I don't think the toys really want
to be actual children
they couldn't bear it

but in their dreams they take flesh
and like kings and queens
feel the sun on their faces
that won't blister their paint
and grow legs that can walk them
through gardens of scented delight

on vesper wings
they go
with no one to see them or remind them
that they are, after all,
only toys
with nothing but toy dreams

the harlequin's farewell party

the toys hold a farewell party
for one leaving the toy box and the pages
of fairy tales
for parts unknown
and adventures inconceivable

the children call it growing up
but of course toys don't grow up, do they?
they only pretend

take Noddy for example – first he was alone
in the dark-dark wood, then Big Ears found him
and since then nothing has changed
he is not just passing through, he is home
under a big never-changing ceiling
with only groundless fears to face

not so the harlequin
with his brightly patched coat
his shredded trews, his bells
and his bare feet
the harlequin has places to go,
people to see
deals to make, vistas to take in
nightmares to ride out

he isn't the type to get stuck in the toy box
forever and a day
riding the little engine that could around and around
seeing the same faces
day in day out
night in night out
until hell freezes over

the hobo steps to the road
heads for new climes
beyond the table leg,
beyond the clatter and the natter
beyond the edge of the door
beyond the edge of sunlight
where the gingerbread man runs
over the hill and far away
up the road and around the bend
neither envied nor remembered
which is how he likes it

in the world but not of it
everywhere and nowhere

the one that got away

you can't say we didn't get fair warning

when the lights are switched off
a glow still filters under the door
just enough to show something
but not enough to show anything

there's only so far you can go
to keep your promises
keep your head above water
show enough but not too much
just enough but not too little

there's only so far you can go
to keep your end of the bargain
to hold it in your heart
to keep it dear to you, like a shrine
to keep it out of the shadows
to keep it where you can see it
to know its partial revelation
like the time in the garden with
the sunwine
and the starwine
and the crispy chips

you can't say we didn't get fair warning

when the light is switched off
what filters under the door is barely enough
to shape the body, desire, hope,
all that Mr Moonlight might bring
on the tripwires of memory

and no matter how far you go
it can never be far enough
from intruders who lurk
beyond the doorway
waiting for you
you who are standing by the toy box
in the half world

waiting

Part Two

out of the toybox

a big backyard

the child peeps
over the rim of the world

wonders await the eye
fulfilment awaits the heart

oh! here are stars that are not
sewn into silk

a moon and sun that are not
painted onto mirrors

people who walk and talk
whose feet move by themselves

and who have large voices freighting
carriages of air

here are windows to the soul
and other places

a big backyard
full of galaxies and radio stars

just beyond the fantasies of
the toy-box child

with his wooden knuckles
and wild, sapphire eyes

these adventures need you

time to set off for
high adventure, tales of the wicked
and derring-do
whether in a pea-green boat
hurled from sea to sea
riding a unicorn with an
iridescent horn
or flashing across spacetime
and other impossible places
in a craft of fine design
the aim is the same
the name of the game doesn't change
in love or war
and the stakes are staggeringly high

heroes are needed
to right the wrongs
to restore
the moral balance of the cosmos
and pluck armageddon
from the jaws of prophesy

it's an old story, always new
as are old lies, always true
and to the hero comes the spoils

the rights to all the songs
and other ephemera

mountains high and valleys low
hobgoblins tall or squat
trolls at the bridge singing
foldewol foldewol
I'm a troll, I'm a troll
with the winter steps of memory
and everything held fragile in a breath
or left behind in the wreckage

the call to adventure
comes dressed in pyjamas
yet cloaked as destiny, heralded by
the cry of a crow or a diamond flash
on a dark horizon – gird yourself, pilgrim
and move out, time is antipathy
and rust never weeps

your loved ones will still be loved
and your grave ones will still be grave
that which is left behind would have been
left behind
anyway
in the long run
that which is in front of you

will come in its own good time
when you will be called upon
to show your mettle
put your life on the line
and bend your head before
the fiery touch of some god or other

time to set out, time to sing the road
fling the wind
adventure doesn't linger for the timid
but chooses the boldest heroes
the most resolute
for the sacred task at hand

is that you or have we got it wrong?

the map is not the territory

the island is limned in black
a shadow image, a history

at first sight, you can't tell what it is
an ink splotch or a rocky dragon
hard to see it as a place where people live
and children play
and the world can seem close
or very far away

I love those old celluloid photos
the tight rolls of negatives
which would unwind
a world full of ghosts
with holes for eyes and bright silver hair

who might or might not have been family

we have these things

we have a beach a sky and garden
a dolls' house
a pretty, vacant space
all anybody could ask
sky-latched, tide-patched, earth-matched
memories patched, most not worth the time
spent making them in the first place

I might just as well have
stayed at home, sailed the winds on a lily
read a book in the panther hours
or whiled away my time in the toy box
between here and let's pretend
with my friends
and pat-a-cake some happy words
pat-a-cake pat-a-cake...

sometimes all anybody could ask
is not enough

I don't complain, I say to people,
but that's a lie – I complain all the time
about this and that and the great injustice of things

the beach salts over,the sky cracks open
the garden floods, the doll's house
gets stolen, the pretty space
crashes
somebody takes a poke at somebody
who passes it on
the toy box fills up with good wishes
as the purse empties

this has to be about as good as it gets

my dad would say

the street scene opens up like most street scenes
cars moving, people walking, shop windows gleaming
words scurrying
all the wind-up toys toddling off home
or catching a train to Toy Town

he's got his head screwed on right
my dad would say
I tried to picture it, reconstruct it,
a whole world built
by men with their heads screwed on right
some with springs, some with cogs
some with bolts and some with braces
and some just stuffed with kapok

the cars stopped moving, the people stopped walking
the shop windows turned to dark glass
and time turned to super glue
at the checkout counter

then the street tipped at some fantastic angle, like
a ship sinking,
bringing the sky and the clouds down
to live among us
while worlds flashed and twinkled in our
well screwed on heads

sister sun and brother moon

side by side they sit
on a mossy wall long forgotten
to listen to the ocean
watch for signs of life, and stare
at the long horizon

sister sun and brother moon
holding hands, linking fingers
joining toes
making amends
waiting for the tide to turn
and the sky to start singing

as their love grows they lean
towards each other, their orbits touching
in the coldest of stellar reaches
their thought patterns merging
into a standing wave

it feels so good

a whisper spreads through
the gathering crowds lining the thoroughfares
those who pray and those who don't
of an impending miracle

formlessness to take form
the birth of a new star
the peeling away of a new cosmos

but nothing happens
that hasn't already happened,
the good moment slips by
like a blessing unseen
and the world doesn't hesitate
even for a moment
to go on its unblessed way

sister sun and brother moon
don't hold their breath
as they wait and love and love
and wait
side by side on a mossy wall
long forgotten

the night stealer

the night stealer sneaks in at night
and steals the world away
steals the sky, steals the stars
steals the moonlit bay

steals all the children too
who might come out to play

imagine, if you will,
an evil Father Christmas
Krampus himself
like a bad elf
who freaks around at the end of the day
stealing
presents from under the Christmas tree
even the sugar-plum fairy
in ballet tights
who stands at the very top of the tree
bearing the light

everything that once shone
becomes pale
and everything that once burst with colour
gets leeched
and everything that once stood forth

disintegrates
and everything that was once full
becomes hollow
and everything that was found is lost

all the things that walk and crawl and wriggle
upon the earth
curl up their toes and shrink
back into themselves

they know what they're after
those night stealers
(they hunt in packs)
they go straight to the heart and soul of things
and proceed to feed
withering the grape on the vine
love in the heart
the song in the bell jar
the whisper of cosmic tides
disposing
what might have been precious
and turning it to dross

oh no, you can't sleep easy
or sleep at all
when the night stealer comes
to steal the world away

in such unlikely circumstances love may be born

the Ferris wheel flies and Li'l Lucy lies
in a pink frenzy of candyfloss
butterscotch fingers
and eyes
too big for her stomach

the organ grinder grinds, the monkey cries
the comedy duo gathers in the laughs
while the melody lingers

Little Boy Lost hides
from the girl with the pink sugar lips
and satin ballet shoes
while the ghost train carries
all the Toy Town toddlers, every last one
into the glad mouth of their screams

Li'l Lucy wins a yellow bear
and wants to go home
she's nostalgic for a world that never was
for kisses that never were
but merely seemed
for the embrace of the bear, and an end
to all the happy lights that make her sad

while Little Boy Lost comes out of
the mirror with not a kill to his name
full of shame
with his jingling eyes
and his fencepost legs
happy to follow her
to the end of the dream

cowboy capers
(for David Gemmell)

sorcerous swords and six-guns -
the lone gunman sets out
across the vanishing plain

where a woman, her two children
and their covered wagon drawn by oxen
are winding their way to Paradise
which always comes with a clear stream
rich soils
healthy children and a good man

it's a big country

presently, a gateway to another world
will open between some standing stones
and demons will pour forth
demons that look like men, demons that
look like beasts, demons
that just look like demons
and they make short work of heroes

will the lone gunman be in time to save
the woman, and her children, and so earn
her eternal gratitude among

the piles of wasted ghouls
or will he be too late and find them
their bodies ripped and torn apart
by a hatred too vast for the human heart?

for her part, the woman's already had one man
die on her
she can't afford a second
wandering the Void in search of lost love
and, besides, grief lies like some special curse
on the Deathwalker, Demonslayer
not for one moment can he still
the crying of his heart

not the kind of man you settle down with

the lone gunman arrives at the mountains
the tracks are clear, they head west
into the sunset – knows a rare, quiet moment
with just himself and his grief under the stars

before all hell breaks loose

walking the shadow

Mr Moonlight walks his shadow
up and down the street
over the hills and far away

as he withdraws his will
from the sky and the earth
a new light arises

the ocean catches it
cradles it
turns it into a new day

a searing flame that lifts
from the horizon
to the cowl of night

where you'll find him
Mr Moonlight
walking his shadow

into the west

moments out of the box

these few moments must stand
for all those times we can't
and couldn't ever
spend together, all those things
we can't and couldn't ever do
the words we can't
and could never say

they are just ordinary moments
these few
nothing special and soon gone
but contain all that we were and could
have been
and never will

like the Petrushka doll you had
when you were nine
one moment unpacks another
and another, all moments contained
in the first
so brief it can't be measured
but must include
the scene on the balcony
under the sun
when something might have happened

or the moment on the bus, in the rain
when nothing did

these things lodge in the heart
to reappear on sunny days
or in the dark-dark wood
where there are only owl moments
with owl tears

then the heart might
skip a beat
or two
in remembrance

blossoms

dropping in
from here, there and everywhere
blossoms
from a fresher time

pink and red and rosey
cream along the edges
fresh from the tree, or someone's posy
they can slip through the air
as if on skis, turn corners
and gently flutter when love is near

like angel's tears, too soft to hold
they fall into the world as if it were a wedding
and they were the witnesses

they do not come from here
you know
but somewhere else, somewhere
that can't be named
for in the naming it would become
something other, but you know it
when you see it
that ethereality

that promise made to a broken land
the harbinger of good cheer

you know them, those blossoms
in all their other-worldliness
the only way you can know them
in the springtime of the world
here and there
and somewhere else
blossoms
from a fresher time

memories of an arrow

as the night fades
and the light is lush
nine suns appear
in the early world
competing for the sky

a multiple dawn
around a single horizon
nine eyes opening

a great fear comes
upon the earth
upon those who live
and those who scheme

when these nine suns
meet in the middle
of the air
what a falling out
there will be

our hero steps forward
with his mighty bow
and his golden arrows
and his gleaming hair

and his naked chest
glistening

sky and earth hang
in balance

the bow is drawn
the arrow fitted

the heart steady
the eye in line
muscles matched

those who live
and those who dream
hold their breath

and as the gods look
the other way
the first arrow flies

lullaby

I'll leave this space open for you
Mr Moonlight
I'll leave my door ajar
and when soft rain comes
to touch the world with bliss
I'll know it's you
and who you are

when nothing comes
but the open sky
clear of any scribbles
and there is no rain
in the world of light
I won't mind
too much
I won't hang out
because, you know
I've lots of places to be

but nowhere to go

I'll put a candle in the window
just in case
you can never tell

with Mr Moonlight
I'll leave the gate unlatched
with a note that reads like this

no strings attached
for just a single kiss

I'll leave this space for you
Mr Moonlight
open and asking
feasting and fasting
throwing wide the covers
smoothing the page
listening from afar

and when soft rain comes
to touch the world with bliss
I'll know it's you
and who you are

making it up

the constellations make a pretty sight
strung like Christmas lights on Mars
way up on high, curling
between
memory and makeshift and all the things
we read into the stars

they come down to earth from time to time
like gods are said to do
pretending to be toys, with eyes full of fire
arms full of gifts
and limbs full of spring

sing! they say, sing!

the constellations look just right
all dressed up for the party
strung across the sky
in one great scoop, making patterns
illusive to the eye

the patterns you find
are there because of the looking
projected from within
connecting of the dots on god's waistcoat

otherwise there's nothing there

but hurdy-gurdy

shapes

fashioned in the mind

all good things

it's hard to say goodbye
when the time comes around
to unplug
and put the words to bed

to quit the show
make other arrangements
say all those sorts of things
that have to be said

but always sound sort of empty
in the saying
like a wind-up toy praying

all good things must come to an end
so I've read

all that has been joined
will be broken

that pang in the heart is an echo
of many partings

stillness above, turbulence below

the toy box has come of age
even if the toys themselves have not
and the echo is of footsteps
heading off stage

for the toys themselves it's not
a farewell
but a change of location
to the pre-loved shop, perhaps
where some of the grander figures
like Big Ted and Barbie
might find a shelf at the right height
to sit and stare fixedly
off
into the far distance

I wouldn't read too much into it
if I were you
they are only toys, after all
only good for let's pretend
there's no heaven for them
or hell
no sun, no rain
no jam and toast
no cries, no laughter

they become the story
only if you make it up for them, keep
pretending,
keep offering them a fantasy life
in Toy Town
where they can walk a street
meet and greet
catch a train
and there are and never have been
any goodbyes

now the toy box is long gone
over the rise, under the rain
or filled with dusty old shoes

the valadections have been sung
or spoken

everyone else has grown up
and lived happily ever after

Also by Mike Johnson

Novels
Lethal Dose
Zombie in a Spacesuit
Hold My Teeth While I Teach You to Dance
Travesty
Counterpart
Stench
Dumbshow
Antibody Positive
Lear: The Shakespeare Company Plays Lear at Babylon

Shorter Fiction
Confessions of a Cockroach/Headstone
Back in the Day: Tales of NZ's Own Paradise Island
Foreigners

Poetry
Ladder With No Rungs, Illustrated by Leila Lees
Two Lines and a Garden, Illustrated by Leila Lees
To Beatrice: Where We Crossed the Line
Vertical Harp: The Selected Poems of Li He
Treasure Hunt
Standing Wave
From a Woman in Mt Eden Prison & Drawing Lessons
The Palanquin Ropes

Non-Fiction
Angel of Compassion

Children's Fiction
Kenni and the Roof Slide, Illustrated by Jennifer Rackham
Taniwha. Illustrated by Jennifer Rackham

www.ingramcontent.com/pod-product-compliance
Lightning Source LLC
Chambersburg PA
CBHW030451010526
44118CB00011B/889